ENERGI
INSCRIPTIONS

Other books by Paul Williams:

Das Energi
Remember Your Essence
Waking Up Together
Heart of Gold
Apple Bay
Rock and Roll: The 100 Best Singles
Outlaw Blues
Bob Dylan, Performing Artist (Vols I & II)
Common Sense
Nation of Lawyers
The Map, or Rediscovering Rock and Roll
Only Apparently Real: The World of Philip K. Dick
The International Bill of Human Rights (editor)
Pushing Upward
The Book of Houses (with Robert Cole)
Dylan—What Happened?
Coming
Time Between
Right to Pass

ENERGI
INSCRIPTIONS

Paul Williams

Carroll & Graf Publishers, Inc.
New York

First Carroll & Graf edition 1995

Carroll & Graf Publishers, Inc.
260 Fifth Avenue
New York, NY 10001

Library of Congress Cataloging-in-Publication Data

Williams, Paul, 1948–
    Energi inscriptions / Paul Williams. — 1st ed.
        p.   cm.
    ISBN 0-7867-0204-4
    I. Title.
    PS3573.I4553E54   1995
    813'.54—dc20   95-6239
                                                          CIP

Manufactured in the United States of America

10   9   8   7   6   5   4   3   2   1

for Erik, Sage, Taiyo & Kenta

with thanks to
Richard Parks, Tony Secunda, Robin Rule,
Donna Nassar, Tim Underwood, Sandra Howell,
Herman Graf, Kent Carroll and Cindy Lee Berryhill.

INTRODUCTION

Message to the Young

Don't be distracted by the noise and lights of this world. It is not your creation. Your task is to create your own reality out of whatever materials you find at hand. The way to live by a set of values is to discover or rediscover them for yourself.

ENERGI
INSCRIPTIONS

Fear of truth
is fear of God
and therefore appropriate.

Gentle courage
is the best response.

Vanity is the great oppressor.

Let go like the fire.

Shine without form.

To live and trust in the face of all doubts,
in the face of our fear of loss,
surrounded by our ceaseless feelings of
        unworthiness,
this is the act of love.

And it is in this act
that human beings achieve dignity
and fulfill their purpose here on earth.

Self-honesty
is the essence
of every spiritual path.

If you are confident
of your own self-honesty,
wake up, friend fool.

Self-honesty can't be done confidently.
It requires the courage to feel,
to be uncertain,
to doubt.

Tell yourself the truth about what you're feeling.
And then shut up.

Shut up and open up.

Notice your indulgence.
Notice your guilt about your indulgence.
Do nothing. Just notice.

And if you must do something,
work on the guilt—
not the indulgence.

What we believe, when we see that our behavior
is weakening us (or someone else)—
when we see that we "shouldn't" do this—
is that our guilt will make us stop.

But it won't.

In a subtle, complex, familiar way,
our guilt causes us to keep going—
to keep indulging.

We heighten the guilt
to try to force ourselves to stop,
and that's exactly the wrong approach.

If we can lessen our guilt
we can in time create an environment
in which we feel less defensive
(and therefore have more choice)
about our indulging.

This must be a gentle process,
a patient, persistent process.

The antidote to guilt is self-love.

Some people have no guilt.

They are not saints.

They are psychopaths.

Do not attempt to be cured of your disease.
Do not try to rid the world of poison.

Dispense the antidote.

Pray for the freedom
to love and accept yourself
as you are.

Prayer and work.
These go together.

Pray for freedom, work for freedom.
Pray for peace, work for peace.

This is all we have to do:
Pray and work and love.

Ancient, simple truths.

Why do they scare us so much?

Maybe because they have the power
to separate us
from our protective illusions
and our materialistic dreams.

We cling to money, security, and ambition
like they were father, mother, and beloved.

I'm not saying, "Let go."

I'm telling you that I, too,
am desperately clinging
to my chains.

How to love yourself.

The best way is to actively give yourself credit
for every appropriate risk you manage to take
no matter how small
no matter the outcome.

Notice and acknowledge your own courage.

When you find yourself feeling fear, pain, doubt
acknowledge yourself
for noticing what you're feeling.

"Noticing" means being present with.

It isn't easy to be present with feelings.
We are constantly drawn to the alternatives.

The alternatives are denial
("I'm not feeling any fear")
and reaction
("I've got to do something about this").

Do nothing.

Do nothing,
and then pat yourself on the back
for your perseverance.

Do nothing.

Breathe.

We are especially fearful of political truths.

Stop reading this page right now.

You might find out something you don't want to
    know.

For example: that the war-mongers
are us.

Or that our enemies
are not so bad.

Or that the power
to transform the world
is here in our trembling hands.

Hearts and hands.

This is the most terrifying news of all:

that what I feel and what I do
make the difference.

I don't want to deal with this.

How can I be gentle with myself
in the face of this crushing responsibility,
this hideous, exhilarating potential?

Make me powerless, Lord.

Relieve me of my burden.

I'm not good enough.

This is the lie we repeat to ourselves all day long.

The world we could be creating
calls to us at every moment

But the noise of our self-absorption
protects us from its call.

Patriotism is a form of vanity.

We cling to our definitions, our borders, our limits.

We are in love with our own self-image.

It is such an unrewarding love.

This is a call to revolution.

How can we hear the call?

We must turn down the noise.

We have the power
to transform our reality—
to make a better world
for all who live here.

What stops us is our fear
of misusing this power.

It is a legitimate fear.

Power corrupts.

Self-honesty is the balancing force.

To live and trust in the face of doubt,
in the face of our fear of loss,
surrounded by our ceaseless feelings of
    unworthiness—
this is the act of love.

Our feelings of unworthiness are legitimate.

And yet it is a lie that we're not good enough.

Imperfect as we are, we have to be good enough
for the work that faces us
because there is no one better.

There is no one here but us.

There is no one here but us
to do our work
to transform our world.

Do I believe there is a force in our lives
that is greater than our minds and wills,
greater than our human awareness?

Yes, I do.

I also believe our obsession with naming
(and thereby claiming)
this force
is another expression
of human vanity.

God is other than us, other than all our concepts.

He is not here to do our work.
We are here to do His.

In practice, this simply means
our work succeeds
when we listen to His guidance.

Noticing what you're feeling
—not denying, not reacting—
is one way of leaving yourself open to guidance.

God comes forth from the silence.

What is your relationship with truth?

Are you proud of it?

Or does it humble you?

Shine without form.

You and I have the power
to make a better world.

Let us begin by deciding
to tell the truth to ourselves
regardless of the consequences.

What can we possibly build
on a foundation of self-deception?

Great collapsing castles.

We live in a culture of great collapsing castles.

We have to put on helmets and armor
just to make it through the day.

Self-protection follows self-deception.

The self doesn't mind.

It loves the attention.

Self-importance is our greatest addiction.

Obsessive attention to our own faults and problems
is just as self-important
as pride in our achievements.

I itch, therefore I scratch.

And scratch,
and scratch,
and scratch,
and scratch . . .

Excuse me, were you saying something?

Just a minute— I'm sorry—
I've got to scratch myself again.

Self-love and self-absorption
seem so close
but they're polar opposites.

Self-honesty makes the difference.

It can't be done confidently.

As long as we can remember this,
we can walk the line.

But the moment we forget
we are completely caught up again
in our familiar confusion.

Judge not
lest you be so fearful of judgment
you can hardly breathe.

It is our judgments—
all of which are ultimately
judgments of ourselves—
that make us so defensive.

Trapped in our defensiveness
we can't imagine there's a difference
between self-honesty
and self-flagellation.

Thank God for the power of love.

Love brings courage.

Love brings reawakening.

Love tempts us
and, finally,
persuades us
to let down our guard.

And so we find ourselves
standing naked
in the presence of the Other.

This is the place of no security.

This is the place of healing.

I stand before you
as I really am.
Whether you accept or reject me,
I thank you
for inspiring me
to take this risk.

You have given me

the courage to risk.

You have given me back
my power.

I promise
to use it wisely
this time.

More important, I promise
to notice how I'm using it.

And to notice my fear of my power.

What is wisdom?

I think it means being present
with what's really going on.

Sometimes nothing is going on.

Are we willing to be present with that?

Not even for a minute.

Turn on the television.
Make a phone call.
Go to the refrigerator and look for something,
anything,
to fill the emptiness.
Anything's
safer than nothing.

Why is that?

Because God comes forth
from the silence.

And God doesn't love us.

If He loved us,
He'd listen to our bullshit.

Wouldn't He?

When native peoples are massacred
in Guatemala or Iraq
so someone in New York (or Paris, or Tokyo)
can make money or get elected
what business is it of mine?
What can I do about it?

All my life I've been looking for the good guys
so I can vote them into office,
or send them money.

Maybe that's not the answer.

Maybe there are no good guys.

Maybe there's only you and me.

But if there's no good guys,
maybe there's no bad guys either?

No! Don't tell me that!

There's a limit to how much
I'll let you take away from me.

We are so addicted to blaming.

It must be somebody's fault.

The power of love
is completely irrational.
This is its first virtue.

Its second virtue
is that it scares the crap
out of us.

Third, it forces intimacy on us.

Fourth, it allows us
to stay the course.

Love is a demon.

Just when you thought you were safely dead,
it pulls off your bedcovers.

It gets us in trouble.

It won't be denied.

Of course, we do deny it.

All day long.

And most of the night.

But love sneaks in through the cracks in the pavement.

Love is the answer.

You and I are the question.

I need to say something about modesty.
Modesty means we keep going.
It isn't about how other people see us.
It isn't about how we see ourselves.
It's about staying in touch with that part of ourselves
that is willing to be here and do the work.

Modesty is not intoxicated by good news,
or paralyzed by disappointment.
Self-importance denies, exults, schemes, reacts.
Modesty listens.
It acknowledges the feelings that come up.
It waits for guidance.

The modest person
is willing to miss opportunities

is willing to bear imperfection

is even willing to be misunderstood.

Don't be proud of your modesty.

Be modest about it.

Feel your own vulnerability.

It's scary.

And it smells like springtime.

Love brings vulnerability.

Our response is to try
to get the situation under control.

Finally we succeed,
and we're ready to go on with the loving.

But in the absence of vulnerability,
love is hard to sustain.

It's not fair.

As children, we invent this phrase
to manipulate our parents.

And then it becomes so familiar to us
we come to think of it as being based upon
some great moral principle.

We hold this truth to be self-evident:
that Somebody out there
has the power to make things "fair"

and He's holding out on me.

No one that you or I know would admit
that they believe in a God called "government."

But look and listen carefully
to how we talk and behave
and you might get a different picture.

We believe in fairness
and complain when we don't get it.

We make ourselves dependent
on forces and persons
we neither love nor respect.

And the result is unhappiness.

We must be careful how we choose our Gods.

People who believe
they don't believe in any Gods
need to be especially careful.

Unhappiness is not a curse.
It could even be a form of guidance.

But only, I think, if we're willing to find
a force in the universe that we can respect
        and trust—
and enter into a relationship with it.

False Gods are everywhere.

Every time you pick up a newspaper
or turn on the television
or go to a store
you are exposing yourself
to a barrage of propaganda.

Are you foolish enough to believe
that this doesn't affect you?

We are under siege.

Love, prayer, and work
self-honesty and daily self-renewal
are our only defense.

If we remain modest
they are more than enough.

When our modesty slips
the world crashes in on us.

When the world crashes in on you
do not despair.

Remember to breathe.

Notice what you're feeling.

Let me hold you in my arms.

And if you can't let me hold you

then all I ask

is that you not pretend.

Going through the motions
makes a mockery of the holy spirit.

It kills intimacy.

It leaves us so alone.

Not pretending
may not seem like much to do
in such a hopeless situation.

But it creates a space
for transformation.

How to be present:

Notice.
Do nothing.
Do not pretend.

Wait for guidance.

The question
that you and I are
asks itself over and over again

Sometimes
the answer is so easy:
a kind word
a touch
a message of appreciation

Sometimes
the intensity of the answer
thrills and excites and fulfills us

But sometimes that same intensity
turns against us somehow

we turn against each other
intensely, violently, coldly

hearts filled with bitterness
and complaint

And now the answer
is very difficult

It is so much easier
to nurse the bitterness.

And what was our greatest desire

—the return of that intensity—

becomes our greatest fear.

Oh fear and desire

hate and love

How shall I pry one side of this coin
from the other
and spend it by itself?

I can't.

And it feels like
it's all your fault.

Blame
is such a soothing drink.

Well, no, actually
it's the source of my upset
I know that

But I keep sipping at it anyway.
Why do I find it so attractive?

I guess it's that it *feels* so soothing
even though I know it's killing me.

Kill me softly,
hatred.

I'm too old and tired
for the noise
of love.

Well, no, actually
I'm not old or tired.

I'm just scared shitless.

But I don't like to admit it.

Fear of truth
is fear of life.

And there's plenty to be scared of.

Gentle courage
is hard to sustain
without some kind of help and guidance.

Love is the answer.

But love hurts.

Even God's love hurts.

Damn it all!

Go to hell.

Go to hell with your love.

I have my pride

to sustain me.

Oh God
if You do exist
help me to be patient and calm
as I try to find my way out
of this house of mirrors.

I see my own failings
my indifference
my laziness
my impatience
my intolerance
in every loving face.

I must remind myself
again and again
not to linger on any of these images
to take one step at a time
and to acknowledge myself
for my courage
in this difficult situation.

Indulging
means giving in
in "little" ways
to the habits of mind
that imprison us.

I'm gonna stop this indulging
we always say
as soon as I get out
of this prison.

Start now.

Start small.

Be gentle with yourself.

Stay the course.

Perseverance
brings success.

Impatience
is what slows us down
every time.

But please distinguish
between patience
and self-indulgence.

Don't be too patient
with your own bullshit.

Be patient with yourself.

There's a difference.

Break the pattern.

Cross the street at a different place.
Wait when you would normally act.
Act spontaneously when you would normally wait.

Swim upstream against your habit patterns.
This is a useful technique
for reencountering the truth of your situation.

Our minds fall into patterns of thinking.
Our bodies fall into patterns of movement—
familiar responses.
This makes the world a less scary place.
It is our defense against the unknown.

We falsify reality
so that we can live, think, and function
in the face of the horror
of the unknowable.

Our ability to do this
allows us to survive
in the world as it is.

I admit it:
we *need* to lie to ourselves
just to get through the day.

Fear of truth
is common sense.

Survival
is a perfectly appropriate motivation.

The habits of mind
that keep us functioning
serve us very well.

And on the other hand
it isn't always appropriate
to get through the day.

Time to die.

Time to be destroyed.

Time to be reborn.

Truth means, "what is."

Break the pattern.

Spend a few moments
with the horrifying, naked simplicity
of what is.

This is a healing process.

Daily renewal—
course correction—
is what allows us to stay the course.

You are the person who has done these things.

You are the person to whom these things have happened.

It is the way it is.

I'm sorry.

When you have the courage
to be this person that you are—
vulnerable, imperfect, uncertain—
you will find yourself open
to love and guidance.

You will and you do.

The process is happening now.

Truth is here for us now.

And fear is our helper

like a shadow

that encourages us to turn around

and face the source of the light.

The light is blinding.

And that's all right.

Close your eyes.

Open yourself to truth
and it will enter through your pores,
your aura, your breath.

It doesn't have to reach you through your mind.

Open your heart.

I don't mean with a knife.

The most direct route to your heart
is through your breath.

Breathe the truth
into your lungs
and trust your arteries
—over which you have no conscious control—
to circulate truth
throughout your being.

No conscious control.

How many times do we think
to thank
our involuntary nervous system
for the tireless miracles
it works on our behalf
each day?

Send a prayer of thanksgiving
to your solar plexus.

Breathe.

Do not pretend.

Do not pretend to understand.

Let yourself feel
the awe
of this moment.

It is not a special moment.

It is a very ordinary moment.

That's the most amazing thing.

Modesty
reminds us
that we're not so important.

Peace, happiness,
and the ability to be kind
depend on
this realization.

Vanity is the great oppressor.

To live and trust
in the face of all doubts
is the act of love.

God
is the name we give
to the terrifying, beloved, incomprehensible force
that reawakens our modesty
and sets us free.

Turn around.

The power
to transform the world
is here
in our trembling hands.